NANOOK AND NAOYA
The Polar Bear Cubs

written by
ANGÈLE DELAUNOIS

photography by
FRED BRUEMMER

translation by
MARY SHELTON

ORCA BOOK PUBLISHERS

TABLE of CONTENTS

December: The den — 6

January: The birth — 8

End of February: Life in the den — 10

Mid-March: The outside world — 15

April to July: The spring of the seals — 20

July to September: The summer of waiting — 26

End of July: Abandonment — 32

October: Cape Churchill — 36

November: Master Fox — 45

Glossary (of words in italics) — 48

*To Irene,
for a shared childhood and
for understanding, always.*

December: The den

All wrapped up in her soft fur, the she-bear is dreaming. Rolled into a ball with her nose hidden behind a paw, she is sleeping deeply, hidden away in her cocoon of snow.

Outside, the storm is raging. Furious winds whirl eddies of snow and veil the huge plain in a shifting white blizzard. The bare trees that stretch out along the landscape like sentinels clutch at the rocky soil with every one of their roots. They've seen worse!

Cold rules like a cruel master over this northern Manitoba region in which Hudson Bay outlines capes and coves sculptured in ice.

In the den the temperature is bearable. That is not to say it is warm there, but the sleeping animal is well protected from the biting winds. The heat given off by her body keeps the temperature more or less steady at twenty degrees higher than the one that prevails outside. It has already been more than a month that she has been a prisoner in this shelter and has been sleeping there.

At the end of October, she set out to look for the place where she had been born ten years earlier. When the *tundra* began to be covered with stunted, stubborn trees, at the edge of what is called the *treeline*, the she-bear stopped. On the south-facing slope of a little hill she started to dig in the snow. She began with a two-metre long corridor that sloped upward to prevent the heat from escaping. Then, with her powerful claws, she worked away at the frozen, hardened snow to create an oval room three metres long by two metres wide and one and a half metres high. The entrance tunnel became blocked up as the room began to take shape. An air-hole was opened in the roof to let in fresh air.

Satisfied, the bear lay down in her roomy den. Lulled by the wind's wild song and calmed by the blue darkness, she fell asleep for a siesta lasting almost five months.

January: The birth

The bear comes awake: something is happening. Her body is being shaken by regular spasms. Still sleepy, she is barely conscious of the event that is about to take place. *Nanook*, the little male, is the first one to put in an appearance, followed a few minutes later by *Naoya*, his sister. Mother Bear knows what has to be done. She licks her two cubs vigorously with her big blue tongue to dry them as quickly as possible. She then swallows the membranes and the birth fluids.

You could not say that these new-born are very pretty. They do not look at all like the smiling teddy-bears that watch over the dreams of sleeping children. These two little runts, whose frantic mewing pierces the silence, look unfinished. No bigger than squirrels, weighing barely seven hundred grams each and measuring about twenty centimetres in length, they are four hundred times lighter than their stately mother and look ridiculously small beside her. Blind, toothless and floppy-eared, they are shivering with cold. Their scrawny bodies are almost bare, sparsely covered with a thin, white, curly down.

Being born is an incredible shock! Lost in their mother's magnificent fur, the babies moan and weep; they are frozen and hungry. Prompted by the survival instinct, they clamber over her huge welcoming body, swimming like tadpoles on waves of white wool, using their sharp claws to climb up her chest as they are irresistibly drawn to the warmth of the teats, the warmest part of their mother's body. Four teats are waiting. Their little mouths seize hold of them and they stuff themselves for the first time with creamy, rich *milk*. With their little bellies full and huddled up against each other in the generous warmth of their mother, feeling comforted and fortified . . . Nanook and Naoya fall asleep while the bear returns to her dreams.

End of February: Life in the Den

Mother Bear is still lost in her dreams. Nanook and Naoya, however, are wide awake. They are almost two months old and look more and more like the idea one usually has of plump, robust cubs.

During their first days of life they spent their time sleeping, huddled up in their mother's fur. Every two or three hours, they would suckle, all the while humming a strange half-growl, half-purr of satisfaction. Whenever they were cold and began to complain, Mother would come partly awake and, with her white breath, warm up her frozen babies, tucking them into the softest part of her fur and holding them close between her paws.

At twenty-six days they began to notice sounds. Their eyes opened when they were one month old. Their little round bodies became dressed in thicker fur.

Now Nanook and Naoya weigh almost seven kilos. They are sleeping less. They move around in the den and play, climbing up on their mother's sluggish body, tobogganing down her shoulders and her back. Like excited, clumsy puppies, they egg one another on, jostle and roll on each other and wrangle, growling with joy. When tiredness hits them, they fall asleep entwined, leaning against the warm shield of their mother's body.

Although she feels lethargic and is saving her strength as much as possible, the she-bear is indulgent. At the slightest alarm she is able to wake up suddenly and, within a few seconds, change into a Fury to protect her young. But all is quiet. She contents herself with doing a little housekeeping, covering the ground with a clean layer of snow when it becomes dirty. The rest of the time she sleeps and lets her two rascals have the run of the den.

Mid-March: The outside world

Action stations! The she-bear grunts, stretches out her flabby body, then slowly gets up. With her strong paws she opens up a tunnel to the outside. The *nival chamber*, dark before, becomes bright, revealing its claw-sculpted shape. Soon there is an opening onto the sky and the blinding light eliminates the smallest shadows.

With sheer delight the she-bear breathes in the collection of familiar smells the wind brings her. She hauls herself outside with effort, slips down the sharp slope, plunges her head into the snow and licks a bit of it to moisten her lips, then, tired from these exertions, looks about her. For almost six months she has not eaten or drunk anything nor taken care of any natural needs. She has lost ninety kilos and must spare herself.

Alone for the first time and too frightened to follow her, Nanook and Naoya are whining. Mother Bear returns to her shelter and reassures her babies with a lick of her tongue. The little family calms down and falls asleep. Over it a porthole has been opened onto the wide world.

Two days later the she-bear allows herself to take a short exploratory walk in the neighbourhood. She absolutely has to eat. She scratches at the wind-shrunken snow crust with her claws and munches on the grass and moss sleeping underneath. This meagre pittance will start up her digestive system again and let her recover some energy.

    The cubs are getting bolder. The two inquisitive youngsters appear on the gaping flank of the den and discover the setting for their life: a huge, bare plain that seems absolutely deserted, gilded by a low-lying, chilly sun. Intriguing, unknown smells waft up to them: earth and wood odours, salty exhalations from algae and tides, musky perfumes floating behind small animals . . . No, that desert isn't as empty as you might imagine!

    Nanook and Naoya weigh almost ten kilos. With their astonished-looking black eyes, their round ears, their thick honey-coloured fur and their plump behinds, they are as adorable as fuzzy toys . . . but much more active, and driven by formidable curiosity.

For ten days the mother and her young stay near the den. The cubs never weary of exploring outside; for them, everything is a game, everything is a discovery. Bubbling with life, they jump around and gallop on the hardened ground until they are panting. Tobogganing is the game they like best: paws apart, they hurtle down the snowy slopes, on their stomachs or backs, growling with pleasure. Down below, Mother Bear rounds up her wild little youngsters all powdered with snow, panting and intoxicated with their own speed. These joyful exercises have their uses: they develop the cubs' muscles and their resistance and make them very agile.

And then one day it's time to leave! The she-bear leads her little brood straight to the sea. On the thick ice of Hudson Bay she is due to meet the ringed seals who are frolicking on the ice pack. For her, seal-hunting is vital: in this way she will be able to eat her fill and once again build up the reserves of fat that were consumed during her long sleep.

But little paws tire quickly and must stop often to rest. Patiently, the she-bear sits down and offers a comforting little snack to the ever-hungry cubs. To cross the hollows where the snow has accumulated they climb up onto their mother's back. Novice riders that they are, they cling to her beige fur as best they can. At a rate of two to five kilometres a day the little troop reaches the shore in less than a week.

April to July: The spring of the seals

It's a good year: there are a lot of ringed seals. As they are fat and share the same environment, they are the polar bears' favourite prey. In March and April the females *drop* their cubs on the ice pack. In its unbelievable labyrinth of ice blocks all jumbled together they dig an invisible shelter in the thick snow in which they hide their new-born *whitecoat*. These shelters offer only relative safety since the bears are capable of spotting these *nunarjak* by the smell they give off, even under a good metre of hardened snow.

Nanook and Naoya trot behind their mother. Tirelessly she patrols the ice with falsely nonchalant step, snout to the wind, sensitive to the slightest smell, the smallest unusual sound. Suddenly attentive, she stops, then, a few seconds later, she begins to dig . . . ten, twenty metres . . .

She jumps up and lands with all her weight on a pile of snow that at first glance did not seem to be anything special. The female seal and the baby she was nursing in the intimacy of her nunarjak die immediately, crushed to death.

In a powerful grip the she-bear drags her victims a few metres away, rips them open with her razor-sharp claws and calmly settles down to eat. Her incisors work like knives. She licks up a little blood, samples a few entrails, but especially enjoys the yellowish *lard* with which her prey is covered. Ten or fifteen kilograms of fat at a single meal aren't about to frighten her! What remains of the carcasses is abandoned on the ice but is not wasted for all that, since a flock of ravens has already spotted it.

Satiated, the bear starts to groom herself. Her oily fur must always be very clean to remain waterproof. She rinses her paws in a water hole and carefully licks herself over and over until she is satisfied. The two cubs sitting nearby have not missed a single bit of the whole procedure. Their training is only just beginning.

Breaking in a nunarjak is almost a piece of luck! Fortunately it is not the only way to catch a seal. The mother bear must teach her cubs the two main techniques that will guarantee their future survival: ice hole hunting and stalking.

In order to breathe between dives the ringed seals dig several *aglu* in the ice pack, which they maintain regularly with their sharp claws so that the ice does not block them. These breathing holes are visited in turn. Guided by her sense of smell, the bear locates an aglu. She knows that a long period of *immobility* lies ahead of her. In her language of grunts she commands her cubs to keep still nearby, without moving so much as a whisker.

Silence is vital: the seal is mistrustful and, if it hears the slightest suspicious noise, it will go elsewhere, far from danger, to catch its breath. The bear settles down beside the hole, with all her senses on the alert. Momentarily she expects to see a little round head with big moist eyes pop up. With a swipe of her paw she will shove the seal against the side of the ice and will seize it in her mouth so powerfully that it will die even before it has caught its breath.

   In the hole a dark spot blurs the green water. The bear gets ready to strike. Just at that moment Nanook decides to stretch his legs and gallops away. Warned, the seal disappears into the protection of the ocean. Missed! Mother Bear is furious. With a sharp threatening growl she summons the careless cub who is gambolling on the ice. She has never spoken to him in that tone and he realizes that he has been stupid. With his ears low and practically crawling, he comes back toward his mother who greets him with a good clout . . . You don't learn to be patient in a single day!

    Spring is coming to an end. On the huge bay the ice pack is cracking all over like a worn-out coat and is breaking up into millions of pieces. In June the sun does not even pretend to disappear and is satisfied with keeping watch on the horizon while it unleashes a parade of changing colours in the sky.

    It is *moulting* time for the ringed seals and time for the bears to go stalking. The weary, lethargic seals haul themselves up on the ice near water holes and take advantage of the long hours of sunlight to renew their fur. They spend their time sleeping and scratching vigorously, rubbing themselves as best they can against the edges of the ice blocks to scrape off their old worn hair and groaning mournfully with frustration when their bodies itch too much.

    The bears benefit from this period when the seals are less vigilant by practising *utoq* hunting. Mother Bear does what the others do. Stationed nearby, the cubs watch carefully. About two hundred metres away a seal is stretched out full length on the ice. From time to time he lazily lifts his head, looks around and then, satisfied, falls into a deep sleep again.

Absolutely silently the half-crouching she-bear takes advantage of the times when her prey is not alert to creep up on it. Whenever it seems about to move, she hides behind ice blocks or simply stops, perfectly motionless, while her light fur blends into the surroundings. The seal, who does not have good eyesight, is unaware of the bear's advance, when in reality death is stealthily creeping up on it.

When the huntress is ten metres away, she decides to try her luck and, with all her strength, rushes toward the sleeping *pinniped*. But her prey has more experience than she imagines and flops into the water at the very moment she is about to seize it. Claws dig into the seal's back, slashing it deeply. Was it too soon or too late? It's hopeless! The she-bear becomes angry and in a rage hammers the ice with her big paws. This time the cubs keep still. No one can accuse them of anything. But the lesson sinks in and they understand that patience, skill and planning guarantee their survival.

Not all the hunts end this way . . . all "sealed" up! The bear is a good hunter and one time out of three she tracks her prey successfully. Summer can come now, as she has recovered her strength and once again put on all the kilos lost during her long winter sleep.

July to September: The summer of waiting

Pushed by the north winds, what remains of the ice pack is scattered in blocks of ice on the ocean towards the southwest. Scattered too are the seals who fish off the coasts in the mild season.

All the bears have gone back to dry land. In late fall, when the cold will once more imprison the bay in its shackles of ice, they will set off again to chase seals. But from now until then they have to be satisfied with the meagre pittance that the northern summer grudgingly offers to the largest carnivore on earth.

Some adult males gather in little groups near the bay. In the cool, damp sand or in persistent snow patches, they dig beds, lie down in them and doze for several weeks, overcome by the heat and ringed about with voracious insects. Moving as little as possible, they live on the dozens of kilograms of fat they have accumulated during their solitary winter and spring expeditions. When it becomes really too hot, they lie on their backs with their four paws up in the air, dispersing their heat more easily this way.

Mother Bear is cautious. Amongst these groups of big, sprawling males, who look deceptively good-natured, it is not rare to come upon irascible or starving ones who attack the young ignorant bears, disembowelling them with a single swipe of their claws and then eating them. She knows that her cubs' little paws are not fast enough to escape from these *mastodons*. Therefore, she avoids the beaches and the little islands off the coast and disappears about twenty kilometres into the back country.

There is no question of her going to sleep on her fat. Even if the warm season is not synonymous with abundance, it nevertheless offers a good variety of edibles to nibble at. For the cubs that knowledge will make all the difference when lean years come to the ice fields.

On the tundra the bushes are laden with small wild berries, red, black or blue ones. The silvery grass, dancing in the wind, shelters a large number of birds who hide their nests on the ground. The ground squirrels and voles feverishly pile up provisions. The lemmings flirt wildly and reproduce at top speed. The multiple streams of melted icewater flow together to become wide, calm lakes where the water birds scatter their long wing feathers as they moult.

Sometimes the sea casts up the carcass of a beluga, a walrus or a whale. Left behind by the tides on the foreshore, little fish and shellfish are imprisoned in puddles of salty water. Ropes of seaweed trace their *arabesques* on the beaches while a crowd of birds circles above the waves. Birds, eggs, small or large mammals, berries and various plants . . . the bear teaches her cubs that they should not turn their noses up at anything.

    The cubs learn a great many things and become very skilful. Naoya has no equal for tracking down the nests of eider ducks who hide their big olive-green eggs beneath bunches of grey down. She also adores the willow ptarmigan's warm eggs tucked away in the greenery. She sometimes ventures as far as the colonies of terns, but the latter do not hesitate to dive down on the intruder, aiming for her big head with their long pointed beaks. This is not designed to hurt her but is annoying enough to make her turn back.

    For his part Nanook prefers the birds themselves to their future offspring. With his snout in the air, he invariably discovers the groups of oldsquaw ducks and snow geese who are waiting for their long wing feathers to grow again, as they swim out on the deceptive safety of the lakes. He tries, without much success, to track the wild, quick-moving big birds.

    The inseparable trio spends the summer walking from one spot to another, looking for little creatures to hunt. The cubs never stray very far from their mother. They sleep close to one another, warmed by the affection that ties them together, in the cool autumn nights that are becoming darker and longer with each day.

End of July: Abandonment

Two years have gone by. The little family has been lucky as nothing tragic has happened to it. The time has passed quietly . . . with its successful hunts, its days of hunger, its sad or funny adventures and its long, peaceful resting periods. Nanook and Naoya have become two-and-a-half-year-old adolescents. For his age Nanook is strong and solidly built; he weighs about ninety kilos and, standing on his hind legs, he is already more than two metres tall. Naoya is lighter than her brother, with a pretty, delicate, triangular head. She does not have Nanook's strength, but she is lively, quick and surprisingly skilled at hunting.
    Since their birth the youngsters have been living under their mother's comfortable supervision. For a year they barely left her side, perpetually famished cubs always after her teats, listening to her grumbling, being schooled by her slightest gestures, delighting in her caresses. Through her they have learned about the richness of the seasons and the meaning of the signs written in the sky, the sea, the earth and the snow. Thanks to her they have known love: that wise, sheltering presence that allowed them to be as daring as they liked, making them almost invincible.

 After the cubs are weaned, although they remain very close, they have learned to keep their distance. Mother Bear has one last gift to give them: she will teach them how *precarious* everything is in this huge cold kingdom where only the strong and the wisest survive. Only her departure will convince them of their own fragility.
 One day then Mother Bear suddenly goes away forever, leaving her adolescents to make their own decisions and live free. Once again she is ready to give birth and must take advantage of the autumn to preserve her store of fat so that she can guarantee the survival of the tiny babies who will appear in the muffled silence of her den.
 This abandonment makes Nanook and Naoya very bewildered. Forever deprived of their mother's protection, the two orphans stay close together, as if they were frightened by the idea that they might lose each other too. They offer comfort to one another and together become used to their newly-found independence.

October: Cape Churchill

Nanook and Naoya are inseparable! Driven by hunger, they have finally gone to Cape Churchill as they are curious about mixing with their own kind — those big, mostly male, bears who look so easy-going and spend their autumn lounging around while they wait for the ice on the bay to be solid enough to carry them out towards their secret hunting-grounds.

Nevertheless, the life at Cape Churchill is not restful for the young bears. It is not easy for them to take their place in the rigid hierarchy established by the strongest and cleverest ones. Observed, evaluated, rebuffed and sometimes chased off by the older adults, they often owe their safety only to the swiftness of their legs or their resigned acceptance of what cannot be changed.

It is not easy always to be on the lookout or to have to share what is technically one's own. One day a lone adolescent manages to pull a small dead beluga out of the water and, after dragging it onto the beach, gets ready to enjoy this dainty morsel. A huge bear, the unchallenged king of the band, draws near the feast with calm and confident step. Instantly the young one begins to growl, with his ears and head down, staring him straight in the eyes.

The giant, who must weigh at least three times as much as the other, is not at all intimidated by these displays of rudeness and bad temper. He starts to yawn widely, to the point of almost dislocating his jaw, then, without any more ado, settles down beside the youngster, helps himself to the best pieces and ignores the protesting growls and bristling fur of his dinner companion.

    Things do not always happen as courteously as this. A cantankerous, sick old bear, who has known better days, behaves outright obnoxiously to the young recruits. Misusing his authority in place of his missing strength, he snatches their food without sharing a single crumb. No point in protesting! The rabid old animal cannot stand any confrontation and his paws are still powerful enough to kill on the spot any bold but naive challenger who might dare to face up to him. There is nothing to be done but to abandon the prey and cautiously clear off.

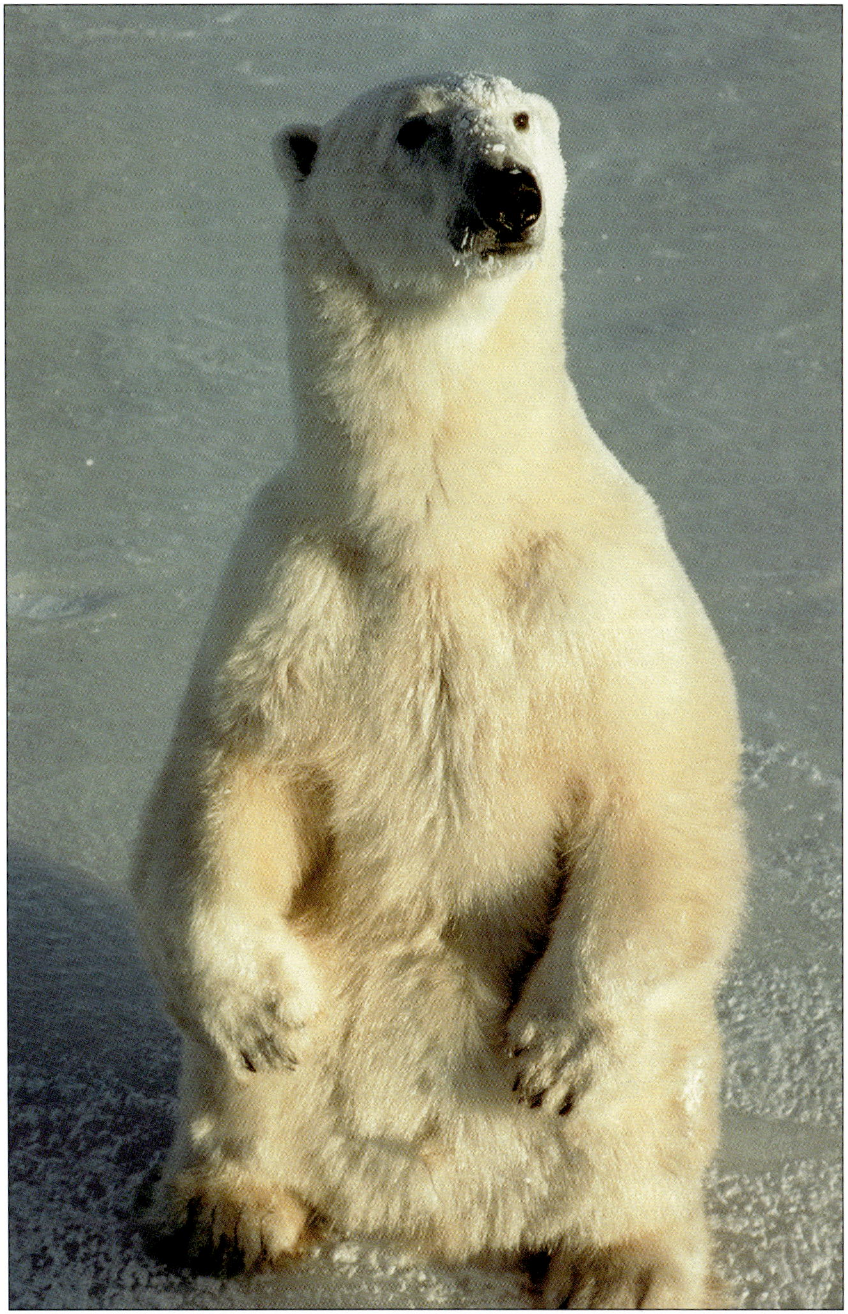

But, on the whole, the big white vagabonds of Cape Churchill are on neighbourly terms. As it is everywhere, the most powerful always have the last word, but, once the situation is permanently established, each member respects the laws of the community. Those who are aggressive and badly brought up are only just tolerated. They are ignored as if they were not there.

Nanook and Naoya are lucky that there are two of them: they are therefore stronger. They hunt and eat together and it is fairly rare that anyone tries to pinch their food. When they are satisfied, they dig a little hollow in the snow and lick each other affectionately to rid their fur of any possible stains. Then, entwined, they lie down side by side to enjoy the show.

For there's lots of fun to be had at Cape Churchill. The seal hunt has been good, the bears are padded with a fine layer of fat and, while they wait for the ice to return, they have nothing to do. Parties are organized. They invite each other to play and dance to tunes that only they can hear.

41

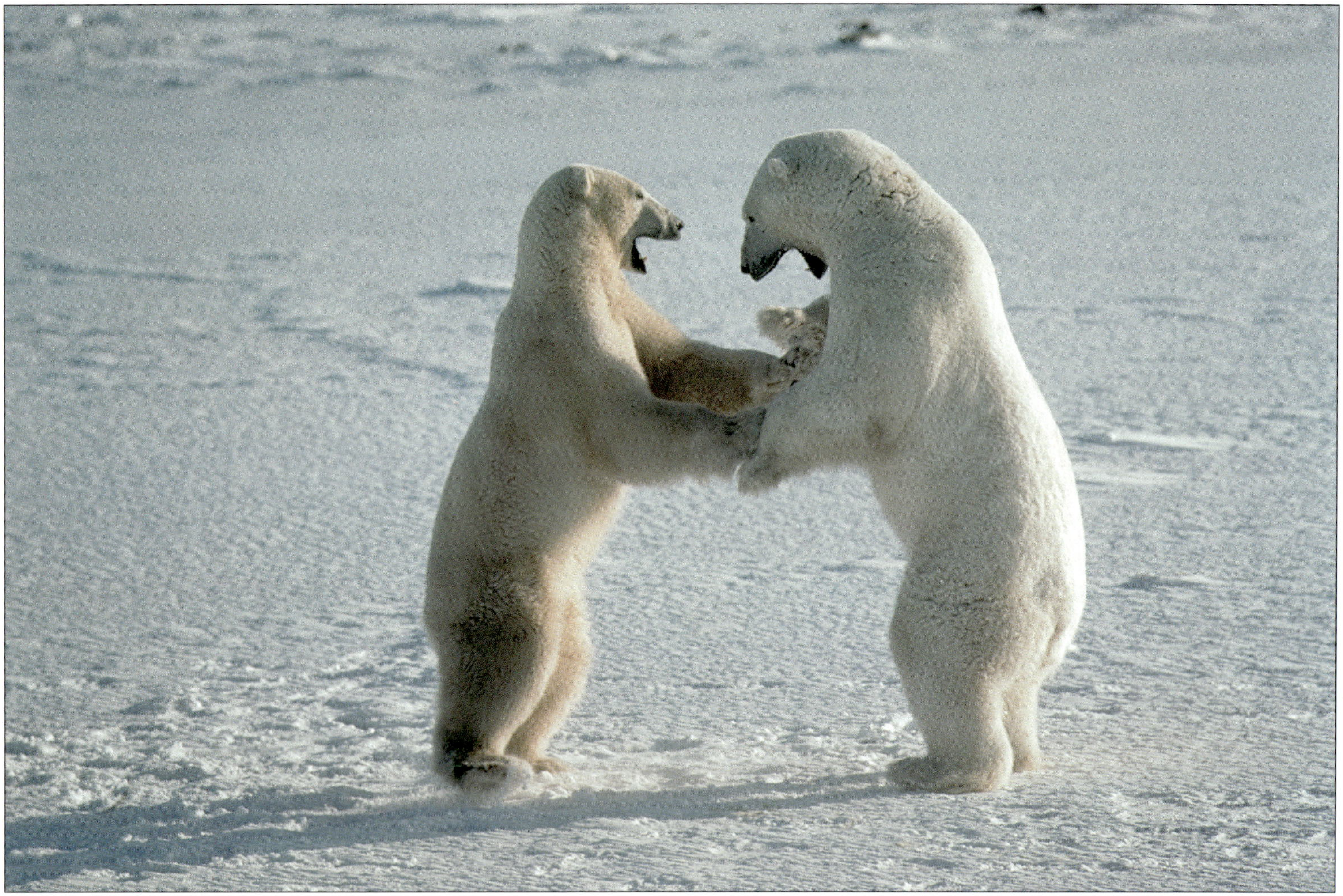

To start a friendly little tango with a comrade, one bear gets up. The two partners look each other up and down, sniff and circle around each other, standing on their hind legs. Then one of them puts his big paw on the other's shoulder. The waltz begins: one step to the right, two steps to the left... Soon, the rhythm picks up: they push and pull and bump into each other... it's real rock-'n-roll! One of the dancers stumbles and finds himself on his back with his paws in the air; the other one falls on top of him — the dance is turning into a brawl. The adversaries roll around in the snow, clasp and bite each other, and grasp each other's throats without doing themselves any harm whatsoever. Only their exhaustion brings them to a stop. They pause, dizzy and out of breath, eat a little snow to refresh themselves, then, at an invisible signal, they again go at their olympic games like giant teddy bears.

The young ones who are too timid, the old ones who are too grumpy, and the leaders who are too sure of their power do not take part in these friendly matches in which each player, without seeming to, tests the strength and skill of the others. When the season of love comes and they will truly have to fight it out to win the favours of a female, the combatants will know exactly how strong their adversary is and will avoid rushing into battles that are already lost.

The cold becomes more biting. The wind scours the plain behind an icy fog, the immensity of Hudson Bay is covered with solid crystal. Serious things must be considered; the hunting season is open. One morning a big male crosses over the beach, stretches out on the new ice to see if it will take his weight, then plunges into the white flurries. One after the other, the impressive white shapes go off into the glacial solitudes. Nanook and Naoya are among the last to leave Cape Churchill.

November: Master Fox

The arctic fox is hungry. For several days now he has not found a decent bite to eat. Flattened on the ground like a shadow, with his nose hidden in his tail's silky plume, he is waiting for his bad luck to pass.

Like a small white bump on the immaculate disorder of the ice pack, the arctic fox is almost invisible. However, the polar bear has spotted him long ago; his sense of smell, a hundred times more developed than a human's, has detected the wild, musky perfume of the little mammal. But Nanook, who is now five years old, has a lot of other things to keep him busy. For several hours he has been sitting completely motionless in front of a seal's aglu and does not intend to be distracted.

Nanook and Naoya have lost one another. In the spring the young female mated with a big, stately male. The following autumn she went off towards the treeline where she was born to fall asleep in a den. In the deepest part of the winter she will welcome her first cubs into the world there, thus continuing the comforting and serene cycle of life. Brother and sister will perhaps meet again, but the understanding that bound them together is gone forever.

Nanook's long, patient waiting is finally rewarded. The water is rippling in the breathing hole. In a few seconds the ringed seal is lying lifeless on the ice. The white fox has missed nothing of this scene. He gets up, stretches and quietly approaches the predator. Absorbed in his meal, Nanook is not concerned with the intruder who sits down a few metres away, but simply growls an unmistakable warning at him.

Like a beggar searching for a crumb, the arctic fox does not take his eyes away from the disembowelled seal whose entrails are steaming in the cold. He is salivating. He really is extremely hungry. Putting aside all caution, he goes close enough to snatch a piece of flesh from the still-warm body. In face of this rowdy's impertinence, Nanook gives an angry whistle and springs toward him. Missed! The fox nimbly dodges him and the bear's big paw grasps only a few long white hairs.

The insolent fellow savours his few stolen mouthfuls and bides his time. He does not dare return to the attack. When the bear goes off to wash himself, the cunning little animal knows that the remains of the seal are his. Actually, this bear is not bad: he's a clever, patient hunter and not too aggressive with starving little foxes... with him, the winter won't be all famine. That settles it, Master Fox "adopts" Nanook!

Out on the inhospitable ice pack that is apparently deserted by all forms of life, the two travellers leave their footprints side by side in the snow, and the bear puts up with this unintentional partner, the *incurable wanderer* dragging him along in his wake. In the creamy dusk of the endless winter days two light-coloured shapes go on their way, step by step, with the little one cautiously following the big one . . . a few paces behind.

GLOSSARY (of words in italics)

Arabesque: an elaborate design

Aglu: (Aglou) an Inuit term meaning "breathing hole."

Drop: to give birth, produce, in reference to animals.

Immobility: bears are capable of remaining several hours or even several days in front of a breathing hole waiting for a seal.

Incurable wanderer: the Inuit call the white bear "Pihoqahiak," which means "incurable wanderer."

Lard: 45 kg. of fat have been found in a bear's stomach.

Mastodon: an enormous person, animal or object.

Milk: a bear's milk is composed of 31% fat and 12% protein, which makes it one of the richest milks among the mammals.

Moult: the partial or total replacement of the shell, horns, skin, plumage or fur of certain animals, taking place at regular intervals.

Nanook: in the Inuit tongue, means "big white bear."

Naoya: (Nauga) in the Inuit tongue, means "seagull."

Nival chamber: another expression meaning "hibernation den dug in the snow."

Nunarjak: an Inuit word used to indicate the den dug in the hardened snow by female ringed seals, in which they give birth to their pup.

Pinniped: generic term designating seals, sea lions and walruses.

Precariousness: the state of something that is uncertain, temporary, fragile.

Snout: a colloquial term indicating a big, round, black nose.

Treeline: an intermediate area between the tundra and the boreal forest (taiga), where sparse woods of stunted trees grow in flatland dotted with clumps of trees and bushes.

Tundra: an intermittent type of vegetation growing in the cold regions, made up of certain grasses, lichens and dwarf trees.

Utoq: an Inuit word meaning "still hunting" or stalking.

Whitecoat: colloquial name given to the new-born of certain seals whose fur is completely white at birth.

NANOOK AND NAOYA
The Polar Bear Cubs

For twenty-five years he has travelled tirelessly all over the ice fields. Every year he has an appointment with the polar bears. He has an answer to every question. His photos are imbued with poetry and light...Thank you, Fred!
All my gratitude to Doctor Jean Piérard.
A. D.

Copyright © Les éditions Héritage inc. 1995

All rights reserved.

No reproduction, publication, printing, or translation of this text by any means whatsoever, whether electronic or mechanical, and in particular by photocopying or microfilming, may be done without the written permission of the publisher.

Canadian Cataloguing in Publication Data

Delaunois, Angèle
   Nanook and Naoya

   Translation of: Nanook et Naoya, les oursons polaires.
   ISBN 1-55143-048-7

   1. Polar Bear—Infancy—Juvenile literature. I. Bruemmer, Fred. II. Title.
QL737.C27D3413 1995 j599.74'446 C95-910516-6

Publication assistance provided by The Canada Council

Printed and bound in Canada

Orca Book Publishers   Orca Book Publishers
P.O. Box 5626, Station B   P.O. Box 468
Victoria, BC V8R 6S4   Custer, WA 98240-0468
Canada   USA

10 9 8 7 6 5 4 3 2 1